Coast

The Coast

of England, Wales, and Northern Ireland

Photographs by

Joe Cornish, David Noton

and Paul Wakefield

Introduction by Libby Purves

Harry N. Abrams, Inc., Publishers

First published in Great Britain in 1998 by
National Trust Enterprises Ltd,
36 Queen Anne's Gate, London SW1H 9AS

© The National Trust 1998
Registered charity no. 205846
Introduction © Libby Purves 1998

Distributed in 1998 by Harry N. Abrams, Incorporated, New York

Acknowledgement:
p.129 Barbara Hepworth, *Carvings and Drawings,* Lund Humphries & Co (1952)

British Library Cataloguing in Publication Data
A catalogue record for this book is available from the British Library.

ISBN 0 7078 0239 3 (hardback)
ISBN 0 7078 0264 4 (paperback, available in 1999)
ISBN 0-8109-6360-4 (Abrams)

Captions compiled by Margaret Willes, the National Trust's Publisher,
with the help of Jo Burgon, Coast and Countryside Adviser,
and Richard Offen, Enterprise Neptune Appeal Manager.

Picture research by the National Trust Photographic Library.
Edited by Helen Fewster
Designed and typeset in Carter Cone Galliard by Peter and Alison Guy
Production management by Bob Towell
Printed and bound in China
Phoenix Offset

Frontispiece: GAMMON HEAD near Salcombe in Devon has all the elements of the great British coast: rocky cliffs, intimate sandy beaches, and glorious waves. [DN]

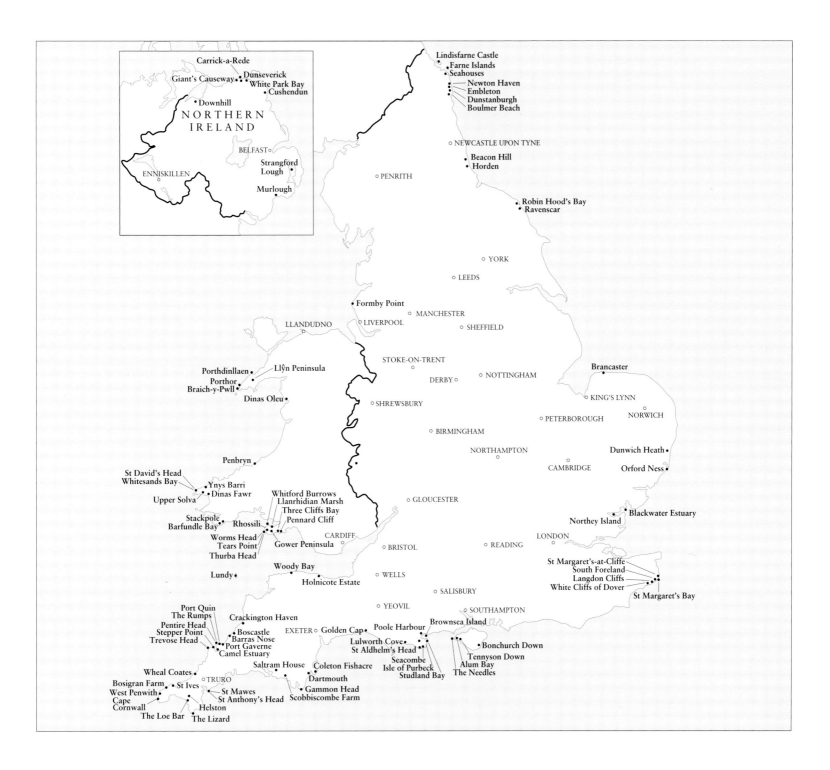

NORTHERN IRELAND

Carrick-a-Rede
Dunseverick
Giant's Causeway
White Park Bay
Cushendun

Downhill

BELFAST

Strangford
Lough

Murlough

ENNISKILLEN

Lindisfarne Castle
Farne Islands
Seahouses
Newton Haven
Embleton
Dunstanburgh
Boulmer Beach

NEWCASTLE UPON TYNE

Beacon Hill
Horden

PENRITH

Robin Hood's Bay
Ravenscar

YORK

LEEDS

Formby Point
LLANDUDNO
MANCHESTER
LIVERPOOL
SHEFFIELD

STOKE-ON-TRENT

Porthdinllaen
Llŷn Peninsula
Porthor
Braich-y-Pwll
Dinas Oleu

DERBY
NOTTINGHAM

Brancaster

KING'S LYNN

SHREWSBURY

PETERBOROUGH
NORWICH

BIRMINGHAM

Penbryn

NORTHAMPTON

Dunwich Heath

St David's Head
Whitesands Bay

CAMBRIDGE
Orford Ness

Ynys Barri
Dinas Fawr

Upper Solva

Whitford Burrows
Llanrhidian Marsh
Three Cliffs Bay
Pennard Cliff

GLOUCESTER

Northey Island
Blackwater Estuary

Stackpole
Barfundle Bay

Rhossili

CARDIFF

LONDON

READING

St Margaret's-at-Cliffe
South Foreland
Langdon Cliffs
White Cliffs of Dover

Worms Head
Tears Point
Thurba Head

Gower Peninsula

BRISTOL

Woody Bay

Lundy

Holnicote Estate

WELLS

SALISBURY

St Margaret's Bay

Port Quin
The Rumps
Pentire Head
Stepper Point
Trevose Head

Crackington Haven

Boscastle
Barras Nose
Port Gaverne
Camel Estuary

YEOVIL

SOUTHAMPTON

Brownsea Island

EXETER
Golden Cap
Poole Harbour

Lulworth Cove
St Aldhelm's Head

Bonchurch Down

Tennyson Down
Alum Bay
The Needles

Wheal Coates

Saltram House

Coleton Fishacre
Dartmouth

TRURO

Seacombe
Isle of Purbeck
Studland Bay

Bosigran Farm
West Penwith
Cape
Cornwall

St Ives

St Mawes
St Anthony's Head

Gammon Head
Scobbiscombe Farm

Helston

The Loe Bar
The Lizard

Introduction by Libby Purves

In 1988, our family set out for what we called a summer's grace: a 1,700 mile voyage in a small sailing yacht, right around the coast of mainland Britain. It was a romantic enterprise and, despite the cold and the wet (it was not a good summer to choose), it became more enthralling and more romantic with every slow mile we sailed, and every small harbour in which we took refuge. By the end of three and a half months, we felt that in an obscure way we owned the place, from the jagged, eternal western rocks and headlands to the low, shifting, mournful mudbanks of the east. We knew the different shapes of the waves, the changing look of the cliffs, the enduring protectiveness of all the little harbours left behind by the age of big shipping. And we were very proud of our coast.

All the way round – and ever since – it has been a source of great comfort in changing times that we do own quite a lot of it; in a sense, at least. The National Trust's Enterprise Neptune campaign was founded in 1965 as an appeal to save our remaining fine coastline from pollution, destruction, and crass development. The Trust has owned coastal property since its foundation in 1895 – its very first acquisition was Dinas Oleu, overlooking Cardigan Bay – but Enterprise Neptune for the first time brought forward the idea that in a crowded, fast developing world, the coastline would always have particular needs and stand in particular danger.

Neptune's first treasure was Whitford Burrows, on the Gower Peninsula in West Glamorgan. Since then, energetically raising funds additional to the Trust's main efforts, it has acquired 570 miles of coastline, and has its eye on many miles more. So cliffs and beaches, headlands and mudflats, simple farms and noble stone breakwaters have come to be recognised, as they should be, for part

The gorse-covered cliff at Dinas Oleu in North Wales, the first property to be given to the National Trust in 1895, a few weeks after the organisation had been founded. Mrs Talbot presented four and a half acres to halt the inexorable spread of the seaside resort of Barmouth, which can be seen to the right of the picture. [JC]

Far left: The rippling sands of the beach at FORMBY POINT in Merseyside. Most of the photographs in this book show the landscape without people, but the Trust welcomes visitors, as shown in this picture of high summer at STUDLAND BAY, Dorset (*left*). [JC]

of an irreplaceable, treasurable national inheritance. The Trust – long a landowner, farmer, and housekeeper – has become a long-shoreman and harbourmaster as well.

One of the strengths of the project has been the Trust's real-isation that it is not only pretty cliffs, sandy holiday beaches and the habitats of birds which are worth looking after. It has these, of course: mile upon mile of them facing every one of our seas: the Gower Peninsula is unmatchable; the approach to Land's End one

of the great paths of Europe; and along the wild North Antrim coast there are sights to compare with any wilderness in the world.

But the works of man matter too, and they matter particularly by the sea, where the great breakwaters and stone harbours left to us from earlier centuries bear witness to one of the most important aspects of our history: the islanders' confident, painstaking determination to reach out into the sea, to send out sailors and bring them safely home. Lighthouses, piers, or whole fishing villages like Cushendun and Strangford in Northern Ireland need as much protection as rare seaweeds or voyaging birds. Otherwise the century of quick-drying cement and fast-buck business would rapidly hide from us forever all that they represent: the values, and the craft, and the lives of our forefathers.

Most surprising of all, to some, was the Trust's decision to buy Orford Ness from the Ministry of Defence in 1993. This is a bleak spot, on the seaward bank of the extraordinary River Ore, which the Trust conserves not only for its rare shingle plants and bird life but for the all-too-obvious leftovers of secret wartime research. Against the bleak winter skylines of the Suffolk coast you can see the 'pagoda' buildings for testing missile warheads and the humble huts where radar was born.

And it is right that they should be kept, to make the Ness a place of sombre reflection as well as aesthetic beauty. For that is part of our history too: alongside the natural history we cherish and the seafaring and shore-dwelling crafts we now find picturesque, we have a right to contemplate the ugliness and ingenuity of more recent warfare. We can watch as its mark on a wild, remote place fades, and the wilderness of sea and shingle takes over once again. It is as much a part of our identity as the greatest sea-cliff or the prettiest estuary.

The coast as an art-form. A detail of the rock face at Strangles Beach, CRACKINGTON HAVEN in Cornwall. [JC]

There are many contenders for the quintessential National Trust coast, but if history has anything to do with it, then Wales can claim the prize. The first property to be acquired by the Trust, weeks after its formation in 1895, was Dinas Oleu, overlooking Cardigan Bay (p.7). The first coastline to be acquired by Enterprise Neptune, the National Trust's coastal appeal launched in 1965, was Whitford Burrows on the GOWER PENINSULA in West Glamorgan.

The Gower combines two vital criteria: its golden beaches, duneland, salt marshes and rocky headlands are of great natural beauty; it also represents an important 'green lung' for Swansea and the urban population of South Wales. *Previous page*: Pennard Cliff on the Gower, looking towards Three Cliffs Bay. [JC]

The Gower, running fourteen miles from east to west, and seven miles from north to south, has Cefn Bryn as its central ridge. Northwards a gentle plateau drops to the shore. Here lies LLANRHIDIAN MARSH, an open area of saltmarsh commonland, grazed by sheep and wild ponies, the winter roost of waders. *Above*: The Loughor Estuary, on Llanrhidian Marsh. [JC]

Right: The western part of the Gower is dominated by RHOSSILI DOWN. Just south of Rhossili village can be found a rare example of a medieval open field system. The Vile, thought to come from the Old English for field, is divided into narrow strips, enclosed by stone walls or high earth banks. [JC]

: 16 : The wide expanse of RHOSSILI BEACH, a favourite for surfers and hang-gliders. The more intense yellow section below the Down is a dune system known as the Warren, which covers a lost village, abandoned in the early fourteenth century, probably as a result of economic decline and the gradual encroachment of the sand. [JC]

WORMS HEAD is a mile-long finger pointing west from Rhossili. At low tide it is possible for walkers to go from Inner Head to Middle Head, and then on, via the Devil's Bridge, a natural limestone arch, to the Outer Head. At high tide the sea swirls round each outcrop so that all that breaks the surface are the head and humped coils of the *wurm*, Old English for dragon or serpent.

Above: The view from the Outer Head, looking towards the mainland. For centuries sheep have winter grazed on the Inner and Middle Heads, which is said to account for their excellent flavour. [JC]

Right: From Rhossili and Worms Head, the coast turns east to Tears Point and the limestone outcrop of THURBA HEAD, a majestic headland 200 feet in height with an Iron Age fort on its western flank. [JC]

STACKPOLE in Pembrokeshire was a great coastal estate belonging to the Scottish Earls of Cawdor. The Cawdors dammed the valleys to create three lakes meeting above the sandy beach at Broad Haven, a man-made landscape of great beauty. But the sea-cliff landscape is equally beautiful, and natural, providing a habitat for the huge breeding population of sea birds – auks, kittiwakes, fulmars and gulls. In February 1996 the birds and marine environment on this coast were badly affected by the oil spill from the tanker, *Sea Empress*. Although National Trust staff and volunteers helped to clean the birds and the beaches, the long-term implications are still being closely monitored.

Above: Looking out from Stackpole south-east to Mowingword. [JC]

Right: The spectacular cliffs are used for rock climbing from the Outdoor Pursuits Centre based at Stackpole. [JC]

: 22 : The headland of DINAS FAWR looking towards the islands of The Mare, Green Scar and Black Scar. This is an exposed site, with the wind and weather keeping the vegetation low. In the foreground the purple sheen on the gorse is a symbiotic plant, dodder. [JC]

The National Trust began to acquire parts of the beautiful Pembrokeshire coast in 1939. At first scattered pieces of the jigsaw were bought, and then gradually linked up, providing a stretch of over fifteen miles of rugged cliffs, inaccessible coves and sandy bays. Walkers on the coastal path can observe large colonies of sea birds and, offshore, basking dolphins and porpoise.

Above: ST DAVID'S HEAD and the ancient field systems of Carn Llidi. [JC]

Right: WHITESANDS BAY, looking south-east to Porth-Clais. [JC]

Above: UPPER SOLVA. The area around Solva is rich in archaeological remains. Some of the Neolithic flints found here show evidence of man's habitation for the last 4,000 years. Four of the ramparts of the Iron Age Fort of Castell Penpleidiau are still clearly visible. [JC]

Right: YNYS BARRI where the Trust owns two miles of the coastline between Abereiddy and Porthgain. This area is characterised by its beaches of grey sand, from fine particles of slate pounded by the sea. The harbour is known locally as Blue Lagoon because the clear waters are turned Mediterranean blue by the reflection from its slate walls. [DN]

PENBRYN, on the Ceredigion coast. The beaches here are particularly suited to bathing and family holidays. [JC]

Behind the little bays are wooded valleys with running streams – it is important that the Trust looks inland whenever possible, and protects the hinterland as well as the coast itself. [JC]

Previous pages: The wide estuary of the Dwyryd at HAFOD-Y-WERN combines extensive saltmarsh with outcrops of rock that are almost gorge-like, and a valley of grassland and oak woods. Formerly this was the site of the Cooke Explosive Works, established in 1865 to produce gunpowder for quarrying slate. Part of the Ffestiniog railway can be seen: this line transported Welsh slate to furnish roofs all over the world. [JC]

The National Trust is helping to ensure the protection of this spectacular estuary and is currently negotiating for the purchase of a large holding through an appeal to Enterprise Neptune donors.

Above: The tiny village of Porthdinllaen on the LLŶN PENINSULA can be reached only along the shore. While the National Trust may own considerable areas of coast, the sea-bed belongs to the Crown: the boundary is at high tide level. At Porthdinllaen the Trust, as harbourmaster, has leased the seabed.

PORTHDINLLAEN'S days as a commercial fishing village are over, but in earlier times it was contender for bigger stakes – the packet steamer trade to Ireland. Holyhead carried off the prize by one vote in Parliament, though it is still darkly maintained that the geological samples that clinched the decision really came from Porthdinllaen. [JC]

Right: BRAICH-Y-PWLL, on the western tip of the Llŷn, with Bardsey Island in the far distance. The north and south coasts of the Llŷn Peninsula are totally different in character: rocky and rugged on the north, long stretches of sand on the south. The peninsula itself has always been farmed, with small fields divided by stone walls known as *claddau*. John Leland, visiting this area in the 1530s, wrote that 'Al Llene is as it were a pointe into the se', and remarked on the doubling up of fishing and agriculture, with the farmers growing corn by the shore and on the upland. [JC]

: 34 : PORTHOR, known as Whistling Sands, from the screeching sound made by the dry sand when trodden on. The small sandy bay is backed by low cliffs rich in wild flowers, particularly orchids. [JC]

: 36 : MURLOUGH, on the coast of County Down, was Northern Ireland's first national nature reserve. In the foreground are the sand dunes, which the Trust has planted with marram grass to make them stable. In the distance can be seen the dramatic outline of the famous Mountains of Mourne which, according to the traditional song, 'sweep down to the sea'. [PW]

Right: Murlough is part of a large sand dune system which built up across the head of Dundrum Bay at the end of the last Ice Age. Evidence of man's settlement has been found from Neolithic times onwards. Seven hundred years ago the Normans introduced warrens of rabbits for their meat and fur, and thus determined the nature of the vegetation: intensive grazing has produced a short turf rich in wild flowers, such as the pyramidal orchid and dune burnet rose, with a few trees and shrubs. [JC]

Far right: The fishing village of Strangford on the western shore of the Narrows on the lough. STRANGFORD LOUGH, over twenty miles in length, is one of the largest sea inlets in the British Isles. In places it is five miles wide, but the Narrows form a bottleneck of less than half a mile where the lough joins the sea, creating treacherous currents. Herring, mackerel, whiting and skate are all fished here, while clams and oysters are farmed on the lough. [JC]

The low flat landscape of S TRANGFORD L OUGH in late afternoon, and (*right*) at dawn. The drumlins, like semi-submerged flying saucers, are deposits dumped by the retreating ice sheets at the end of the last Ice Age. There are over a hundred of these islands and, together with the shoreline, they provide habitats for a huge and varied number of plant and animal species. Because of this wealth, the lough is a marine nature reserve, with the various organisations that own the foreshore working together on a management committee to ensure there are areas of sanctuary. [JC]

The marine nature reserve at Strangford provides habitats for over 2,000 recorded species of birds. Large numbers of duck and goose, including widgeon, shelduck and pale-bellied Brent Goose over-winter here. The muddy and sandy shores provide feeding grounds for large flocks of waders, such as oyster catcher, lapwing, golden plover, curlew, redshank, dunlin and knot. [JC]

Alongside all the wildlife, the lough is used for recreation – water sports, shooting, walking and riding – and for shellfish culture, commercial fishing and field studies. [JC]

: 44 : WHITE PARK BAY on the North Antrim coast. This was the first piece of coast in Northern Ireland to be bought by the National Trust in 1938, with support from the Pilgrim Trust, a charity particularly interested in saving unspoilt coastline, and the Youth Hostels Association.

One of White Park's great attractions is the wide, sandy beach, backed by botanically rich sand dunes. By tradition local farmers have extracted sand for use on their fields, but in recent years this has developed into a major enterprise, depleting the sand and speeding up erosion and starving of the dunes. The Trust has sought to solve this particular problem by providing sand for removal at nearby Cushendun. [PW]

Above: One of the National Trust's interpretation vans, displaying an artist's impression of the extraordinary swing bridge which temporarily joins the island of CARRICK-A-REDE to the mainland. [JC]

Carrick-a-Rede is Gaelic for 'rock in the road', the route taken by salmon each year. At the beginning of the fishing season in April the local fishermen sling the rope bridge across the deep chasm (*right*), and use this tricky access until the season's end in September. [JC]

The GIANT'S CAUSEWAY on the Antrim Coast, a World Heritage Site that attracts over half a million visitors a year. They are following a long tradition, for visitors have been travelling over the centuries to see the huge basalt polygonal pillars that look like giant organ pipes. This extraordinary geological formation was caused by volcanic activity millions of years ago, though legend has it that the causeway was created by the giant Finn McCool to get to Scotland to fight another giant. An echoing fragment of causeway is to be seen at Fingal's Cave on the Scottish island of Staffa. [JC]

Left: The Mussenden Temple at DOWNHILL in County Londonderry. This was built as a commemoration of love by Frederick Hervey, 4th Earl of Bristol and Bishop of Derry, and thus known as the Earl-Bishop. He was also known as 'the edifying bishop' as he loved building, especially rotundas. The rotunda at Downhill was built for his cousin, Frideswide Mussenden, but sadly turned out to be her memorial as she died suddenly in 1785. The Earl-Bishop's vast palace at Downhill is now a ruin, but the Mussenden Temple still perches precariously on the cliffs. [JC]

Above: Fulmars nesting at Dunseverick. In 1921 only one pair of fulmars bred on the north coast of Ireland, but the bird has so flourished that it is now one of the commonest nesting birds on the Antrim cliffs. [JC]

Previous pages: FORMBY POINT, on the Sefton coast in Merseyside, is a remarkable survivor – unspoilt coast close to the urban sprawl of Liverpool. Five hundred acres (200 ha) of sand dunes, created as the Crosby Channel silted up and the sea receded, are now home to a range of unusual plants, due to the sweepings from grain cargoes discharged at Liverpool. The National Trust is working with the local council, and financial aid from the European Community, to stablilise this fragile coastline by planting marram grass on the dunes. [JC]

Right: Behind the sand dunes at Formby are several former dumps for nicotine, brought here from tobacco processing factories on Merseyside. Pine forests, planted at the beginning of this century, again to stabilise the site, are now one of the last strongholds of the red squirrel in Britain (*above*). Their more aggressive grey cousins have been sighted only four miles away, although the National Trust has implemented various initiatives to try to keep the red squirrel safe. [JC]

: 56 : LINDISFARNE
CASTLE rises up on a
basalt crag, accessible
only at low tide by the
causeway to Holy Island.
The castle was built in
Tudor times to protect
the Northumbrian coast
from possible French
attack, but its present
form dates from the
beginning of this century,
when Edward Hudson,
founder of *Country Life*,
decided to make it his
summer retreat. The
architect Edwin Lutyens
turned the primitive fort
into an attractive home,
though even he could not
give it all the comforts.
Lytton Strachey, staying
on Lindisfarne in 1918,
wrote to a friend, 'All
timid Lutyens – very
dark, with nowhere to
sit, and nothing but
stone under, over and
round you, which
produces a distressing
effect – especially when
hurrying downstairs for
dinner – to slip would
be instant death.' [JC]

Above: A rock pool in the marine nature reserve at NEWTON HAVEN, Northumberland. The water here is particularly clear with heart urchins and a rich gathering of molluscs and crustaceans. [JC]

Right: Fishing boats at SEAHOUSES. This photograph was taken in 1989, when there were twice as many boats as today. The traditional east coast cobles fishing for salmon, sea trout, cod, lobster and crab are sadly dwindling in numbers. Some boats are licensed by the National Trust to take visitors out to the bird sanctuaries on the Farne Islands. [JC]

The FARNE ISLANDS came to the National Trust through the initiative of Lord Grey of Falloden, the man who, as Foreign Secretary at the beginning of the First World War, described the lights going out all over Europe. His rousing appeal raised the necessary money and the Farnes became Trust property in 1925. But the twenty-six islands have been a sanctuary for seabirds such as kittiwake, puffins, guillemots, and terns for centuries. St Cuthbert, who lived as a hermit on Inner Farne in the seventh century, laid down rules for the protection of eider ducks when nesting. They are now known to Northumbrians as Cuddy ducks in his memory.

The Farnes are one of Europe's most important nature reserves. The Trust seeks to ensure the birds and the Atlantic grey seals flourish while visitors are shown as much as possible. Visitors land only on Inner Farne and Staple Island, but can see the teeming bird life on other islands from their boat. *Left:* Young shag at the end of their first season. [JC]

Right: Puffins. [JC]

Southwards from the Farnes stands the spectacular castle of DUNSTANBURGH, built on the basalt ridge of Whin Sill, that further west carries Hadrian's Wall. In the middle ages Dunstanburgh was the stronghold of the Earls and Dukes of Lancaster until it was reduced to a ruin in the Wars of the Roses. No roads lead to it, so visitors arrive along the shore from Craster or Embleton. [JC]

The castle is now home to seabirds like the kittiwake (*above*). [JC]

The Northumbrian coast offers both rocky headlands and sandy beaches. *Left:* BOULMER BEACH still has the anti-tank blocks, put up in the Second World War rather than to prevent the gin smuggling, which apparently was a thriving trade here. [JC]

Above: At EMBLETON there is a sweep of sand backed by dunes which are not only home to wooden holiday chalets but also wild flowers like bloody cranesbill, burnet rose and purple milk vetch. [JC]

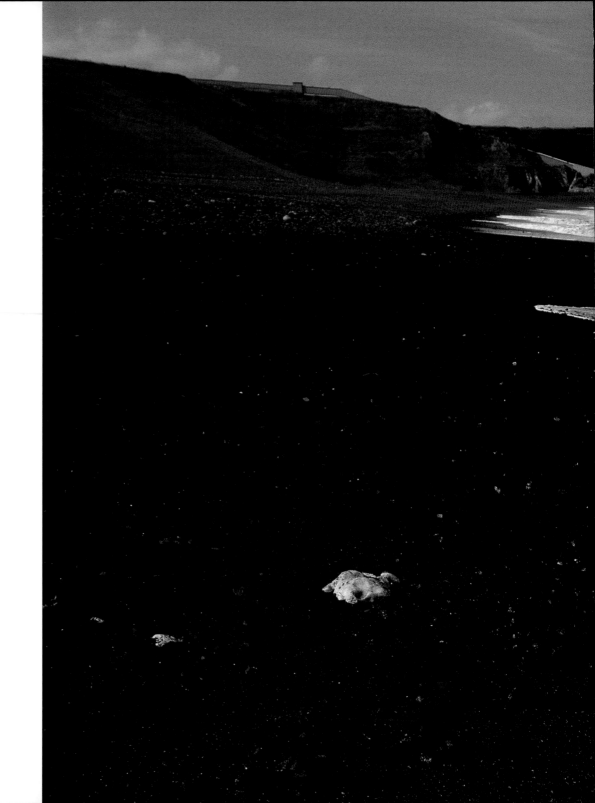

HORDEN on the Durham
coast marks a watershed for
Enterprise Neptune. Before
Neptune was launched in
1965, the National Trust
had conducted a survey of
the 3,000 miles of coastline
of England, Wales and
Northern Ireland. Some
coast was already protected
by the Trust and other
organisations: of the
rest one third was judged
to be developed beyond
conservation; one third of
little interest; and one third
to be of outstanding
natural beauty. Enterprise
Neptune was aimed at
securing as much of this
last category as possible.
  However, in 1988, when
the appeal bought its 500th
mile, it was Horden, where
coal-mining had taken place
under the sea and the slag
thrown on the beach. This
property would not have
appeared on the original
list of outstanding sites of
beauty, but now the Trust
recognised that the area
between the cliffs and the
highwater mark contained
a whole series of important
habitats. This photograph
shows Horden at the time
of acquisition, with its
black beach. Today it
has been restored to its
condition a century and
a half ago with its former
eco-systems flourishing.
[JC]

Left: When the National Trust bought Horden from British Coal for £1, the fields on BEACON HILL, above the beach, were cultivated with wheat. [JC]

Under a Countryside Stewardship Grant Scheme, the Trust has taken away the crops to improve the wildlife on this habitat of magnesium limestone, and to provide public access via a coastal path.

Right: Rock pools on Horden Beach. Following a long mining tradition, visitors still gather coal dust, using it to feed their vegetables, especially their prize leeks, on the cliff-top allotments. [JC]

Right: ROBIN HOOD'S BAY in North Yorkshire, looking north from the cliffs of Ravenscar. The striped effect in the bay is produced by wave action, cutting platforms in the complex geological layers of shale, limestone and sandstone. [JC]

Ravenscar is 'the town that never was'. In the early years of this century a company tried unsuccessfully to create a holiday resort to rival Scarborough. Sewers and roads were laid down, but people were put off by the high winds and exposed cliff-top.

Above: Behind the headland, the National Trust owns a patchwork of farmland, former alum and silica quarries, and brickworks for the town's development, now abandoned. This photograph shows the old brick ovens at Peak Alum Works. Here alum was extracted for use as a fixative in the dyeing of wool. In the nineteenth century the shale was dug out of the cliffs by hand, laid in piles and roasted slowly over a brushwood fire. The residue, brick red, was washed with water and an alkaline solution, usually stale urine supplied by the local population. [JC]

The rock pools below the cliffs at RAVENSCAR (*left*) are of great geological interest, for the coast here is famous for its ammonites and belemnites, primitive members of the family of marine molluscs. Because of their likeness to curled horns, ammonites are named after Ammon, the ram-headed god of the Ancient Egyptians. Local Yorkshire tradition has it, however, that St Hilda of Whitby, finding this area infested with snakes, cut their heads off, and drove them over the cliffs. Their bodies then curled up and turned into stone (*right*). [JC]

Following pages: Ladybirds perching on the reeds in the early morning at BRANCASTER in Norfolk. This is classic East Anglian landscape: the horizons here are low and broad, the shoreline constantly changing through the action of wind and waves on shingle and sand. [PW]

In Anglo-Saxon times Dunwich in Suffolk was the capital of East Anglia; in medieval times it was one of the great ports of the east coast. Today, scarcely anything is left: the low cliffs have crumbled and the great entrepôt has been washed into the sea.

South of Dunwich is the heath now looked after by the National Trust. It consists of about a mile of shore and cliff, together with over 200 acres (80 ha) of heathland, which the Trust's warden maintains by grazing to prevent it reverting to scrub and woodland. It is an important bird reserve and a sanctuary for rare healthland species such as nightjar.

Left: The foreshore at DUNWICH HEATH, looking south to the nuclear power station at Sizewell. [JC]

Above: Silver birch trees, which have to be kept in check to maintain the heathland habitat. [JC]

ORFORD NESS is a narrow shingle spit about ten miles in length, running parallel with the Suffolk coast. *Left:* The saltmarshes and narrow straits that separate the Ness from the main coast, with the fishing village of Orford. [JC]

For centuries Orford has provided shelter from the North Sea. In the twelfth century Henry II built his square keep to protect the harbour. Five hundred years later a lighthouse was erected on the Ness, following a stormy night when thirty-seven ships were lost in the treacherous waters off the spit: this was replaced in 1792 by the lighthouse that is still maintained by Trinity House (*right*). [JC]

The Ness at Orford is the largest cuspate spit in Europe, its estuarial mudflats and the ridges on the shingle created by the wind and waves providing a home for marsh birds like the avocet and the marsh harrier, and seabirds – it supports a huge colony of breeding common gulls – and for wild flowers. With the help of European funding, the National Trust has brought back grazing and raised water levels to reintroduce reed beds and thus enhance the nature conservation value of the area.

Left: Gulls nest directly on the shingle. [JC]

Above: Sea thrift is one of the many plants that flourish in the harsh environment of Orford Ness. [JC]

In this century the flat terrain and isolated position of Orford Ness has been exploited for military purposes. In the First World War it was used by the Royal Flying Corps; in the 1930s trials in radar were carried out here; and in the Second World War, Barnes Wallis experimented with new types of bomb. Finally, during the Cold War huge aerials were erected on the Cobra Mist site (*right*) for a sophisticated defence system gathering information from all over the world – within months of its installation it was already superseded. [JC]

On another part of the Ness oriental-style pagodas were built (*above*) for the testing of nuclear warhead detonators. In the event of an accident, the pagodas would collapse in on themselves. [JC]

In the 1970s the Ness was declared surplus to Ministry of Defence requirements, and twenty years later, in 1993, a five-mile stretch was bought by the National Trust through Enterprise Neptune with the support of various organisations. Many of the buildings connected with the sinister affairs of war remain, adding powerfully to the mournful beauty of this site.

: 84 : Despite its proximity to densely populated areas the BLACKWATER ESTUARY in Essex retains its isolated feel, each farm having its sea wall, saltings and mudflats. At the head of the estuary lies NORTHEY ISLAND, connected to the mainland by a causeway (*far right*). [JC]

In the ninth and tenth centuries, Northey and other islands along this coast were used as hideaways by the Vikings on their forays into Anglo-Saxon England: the bloody Battle of Maldon was fought in 991 between Saxons and Vikings on the site now occupied by South House Farm at the mainland end of the causeway.

Today the National Trust, in association with the Environment Agency and English Nature, is experimenting in allowing the sea to breach the old sea walls, returning the habitat to saltmarsh. This will not only encouarage saltmarsh birds to over-winter, but also provide a buffer to protect other areas vulnerable to flooding. *Right:* Remains of the revetment that originally protected the seaward edge of the saltmarsh. [JC]

The famous WHITE CLIFFS OF DOVER, and of the Kent coast are the result of the North Downs meeting the English Channel. The seas on this stretch of the coast are notoriously treacherous, especially the shifting shoals of the Goodwin Sands. This was recognised by the Romans, who built the first lighthouse in Britain at Dover. On the edge of the downland near St Margaret's stands another pioneering lighthouse, the SOUTH FORELAND (*above*), built in 1843, originally lit by an oil lamp, but later converted to electricity, the first in the country to be so powered. From South Foreland, Marconi made the first contact by radio with the East Goodwin lightship on Christmas Eve 1898. [JC]

Left: Sunrise reflected on the cliffs, with South Foreland just peeping over the horizon. [PW]

: 88 : The chalk of LANGDON CLIFF, just east of Dover, gleaming white in the sunlight, was formed over 100 million years ago from the shells of microscopic shrimps, which settled at the bottom of the ocean. After the last Ice Age this part of south-east England became grassland, while the rest of the British Isles was covered in forest; this has resulted in a number of plant species which have remained local to the area. [PW]

Right: Down on the beach at ST MARGARET'S BAY, where the boulders cluster like huge sculptures at the foot of the chalk cliffs. [PW]

Left: This is the nearest point to France on the British mainland and is the traditional starting or finishing point for cross-Channel swimmers. [PW]

The National Trust looks after eighteen miles of coast on the Isle of Wight. *Above:* BONCHURCH DOWN in South Wight is a coastal heath on chalkland, a habitat very vulnerable to scrub development. The Trust maintains the heathland by grazing with semi-wild New Forest ponies, and with feral goats. [JC]

Left: Paragliders hovering over TENNYSON DOWN on West Wight. The Down was given to the National Trust in 1927 by his son in memory of the Victorian poet, Alfred Lord Tennyson, who walked there daily when living at Farringford. Beyond lies West High Down, providing the final link of the western tip of the island to the Needles. [JC]

ALUM BAY on the Isle of Wight, where the famous coloured sands, running from deep reds to greens and blues, are created by the minerals that have seeped into the chalk.

Left: Looking towards Hatherwood Point.

Right: View of the NEEDLES, three dramatic pinnacles created by erosion of the chalk cliffs. A lighthouse stands on the most seaward, while built into the cliff is the nineteenth-century Old Battery, part of Lord Palmerston's system of defence of the Solent. [JC]

The chalk rocks of the : 97 :
Needles are linked westwards
with the crumbling chalk
stacks of Old Harry Rock
and Old Harry's Wife on the
eastern shore of the ISLAND
OF PURBECK in Dorset.
Purbeck is, in fact, not an
island at all, but a rectangular
peninsula ten miles long by
seven miles wide. It includes
Poole Harbour, and on the
western side St Aldhelm's
Head and Lulworth Cove.
[JC]

BROWNSEA ISLAND represents an oasis of quiet and a sanctuary for wildlife in the midst of Poole's highly commercialised harbour. This character was reinforced by Brownsea's last private owner, Mrs Bonham Christie, who lived here in seclusion from 1927 until her death in 1961, when the island was transferred to the National Trust. *Right:* The lagoon at Brownsea. [JC]

Above: Visitors to the island arrive at the quay, with its coastguard cottages and landing stage in Gothick style. To the left is Brownsea Castle, originally constructed by Henry VIII in the 1540s as part of his revamping of the defences along the south coast, but rebuilt at the end of the last century and now run by the John Lewis Partnership as a holiday home for staff. [JC]

Approximately 120,000 visitors land each year on Brownsea, making their way into the island's interior to enjoy its wildlife. Brownsea is one of the few places where the red squirrel survives, and because it is an island, is easier to defend than the colony at Formby (p.54). It is also a breeding site for terns, visiting waders and wildfowl.

Above: Beach and cliffs on the south east corner of Brownsea. Dredging to enable large ships to enter Poole Harbour has resulted in erosion of the cliffs. The National Trust has sunk huge quantities of stone to break the force of the waves, but the current problem is to know what to do next. [JC]

Right: The northern half of the island is let to the Dorset Wildlife Trust and managed as a nature reserve. [JC]

Right: The last rays of the sun on St Aldhelm's Head near Seacombe on the Isle of Purbeck. This is a highly worked landscape, for the Purbeck limestone has the character of high quality marble, and has been quarried for centuries to be shipped out for cathedrals and palaces. The Seacombe quarries, abandoned in the 1930s, form man-made caves in the sea cliffs, now the residence of bats. [JC]

Far right: Eastington Farm on Purbeck. Sheep grazing the turf encourage chalk downland flowers such as orchids and vetches. A little below Eastington Farm is a man-made rabbit warren, in appearance not unlike an ancient long barrow. As at Murlough (p.38) rabbit farming provided a valuable source of protein in medieval times. [JC]

GOLDEN CAP on the Dorset coast gets its name from the band of green sandstone that glistens as the sun strikes the cliffs, with a view eastwards along the beach to St Gabriel's Mouth with Portland Bill in the background (*right*). Above the sandstone lies a thin layer of cherty soil, and below a bed of blue lias clay, which is often treacherous and on the move, as is demonstrated by the landslip that runs right through the seaside resort of Lyme Regis. This complex geology from the Jurassic period results in an area rich in fossil remains. [JC]

The National Trust has gradually been accumulating its Golden Cap estate and now owns 2,000 acres (800 ha) in one continuous spread. Most of the holding is accommodation land; land without buildings let to nearby farms. *Above:* Farmland on the clifftops looking west towards Seatown and Lyme Bay. This land is steep and hilly, with thin soil, so it is mostly used for grazing sheep and cattle. [JC]

The view from Bossington Hill on the HOLNICOTE ESTATE, looking down towards Bossington Beach in Porlock Bay on the north Somerset coast (*above*). [JC] Since this photograph was taken in April 1993 the landscape has changed as the National Trust has undertaken managed retreat of the bay. As the shingle holding back the sea (*right*) is breached, so the farmland behind Bossington Beach reverts to a saltmarsh habitat. [JC]

The north Devon coast, forming the western extremity of the Exmoor National Park, is particularly beautiful: a landscape of heather moorland, cliffs, deep wooded combes and isolated hamlets. WOODY BAY, (*above*) with its hanging oak woods swooping down to the seashore, has a secretive feel, yet once it was a port of call for paddle steamers plying the Bristol Channel. [DN] *Left:* The stump of a pier recalls its former bustle; now it is the haunt of seabirds like the fulmar and the kittiwake. [DN]

The vulnerability of SCOBBISCOMBE FARM near Kingston, south Devon, has been recognised for the past 25 years; indeed the Trust has made three previous attempts to secure it from development, each failing for lack of funds. Now, thanks to the generosity of Enterprise Neptune donors, a grant from the Heritage Lottery Fund and a magnificent bequest from the late Mrs Hornby, left to benefit her favourite part of the Devonshire coast, the farm, with its majestic cliffs and wooded combe running down to two remote beaches, is safe for ever. [DN]

LUNDY is the top of an undersea mountain of granite, rising out of the Bristol Channel eleven miles north of Hartland Point on the Devon coast. *Right:* The west side of the island is the most rocky, and peeping out from the highest point is Old Light, a stone tower built in 1820. The fogs of the Bristol Channel obscured its beam to such an extent that ships were driven onto Lundy's reefs. [JC]

To counter this, two new lighthouses were built, the North and South Lights, at the foot of the cliffs at either end of the island. *Above:* Old Light seen through the grave-stones in the churchyard. [JC]

Lundy, England's only statutory marine nature reserve, was bought in 1969 for the National Trust by 'Union Jack' Hayward in conjunction with the Landmark Trust who manages it.

Previous pages: DARTMOUTH looking towards Coleton Fishacre on the south Devon coast. On the left is the day-mark set up by Trinity House to aid entry into the estuary. The Trust early acquired land along this coast to protect it from development of holiday towns, but there are still vulnerable areas: recently a farmer, refusing offers from housing developers, generously gave the National Trust Lower Halsdon Farm on the estuary of the Exe. [DN]

Right: SALTRAM HOUSE, just outside Plymouth, is a handsome early eighteenth-century mansion with rooms designed by Robert Adam and a fine collection of paintings, including several by Joshua Reynolds, born in Plympton and a close friend of the Parker family. The landscaped park lies along Plymouth Sound, with magnificent views over the water. The Trust is following a policy of allowing the River Plym to flood Blaxton Meadow through sluicing, and returning land to saltmarsh to encourage a brackish style of vegetation. [JC]

Cornwall is shaped like a bony finger pointing out into the Atlantic. This gives it a very long coastline, made even longer by inlets and headlands: indeed, Cornwall has more coastline than any other English county. The National Trust protects forty per cent of this coastline, so this could be regarded as the heart of Neptune's kingdom.

While Cornwall's north coast is rugged and exposed, the south coast is much gentler, enjoying a kinder climate, producing a landscape of flooded valleys that provide excellent harbours.

Left: The view from St Anthony Head looking towards St Mawes. The castle set up on the cliff was built by Henry VIII as part of his defence of the south coast against French threats in the 1540s. With its sister castle, Pendennis to the west, it protects the entrance to the deep water channel of Carrick Roads. [jc]

Above: The view in the other direction, looking from Great Molunan Beach towards St Anthony Head with a lighthouse at its foot. This headland was fortified in 1805, the year of Trafalgar, and continued to be manned by a coastal artillery unit until 1957, when the Trust bought the land with generous help from the local community. [jc]

THE LOE is a freshwater lake over a mile long, separated from the sea by a shingle bar. Originally it was the estuary of the River Cober with the port of Helston at its head, but by the thirteenth century the bar had formed, rather mysteriously consisting of flint. Legend, however, claims it as the lake into which King Arthur threw his sword Excalibur. Today it provides a haven for wintering wildfowl.

Left: The Loe Bar that separates the lake from the sea, with Porthleven in the distance. [JC]

Right: Loe Pool, looking towards Lower Pentire, an eighteenth-century farmstead that has been converted into National Trust holiday cottages. [JC]

Previous pages: THE LIZARD is a broad, flat-topped peninsula terminating at Lizard Point, the southernmost extremity of mainland Britain. The two-towered lighthouse was built in 1751, with the light produced by burning coal. The 'overlooker' lay on a sort of couch in a cottage between the towers, using the windows on either side to view the lanterns. If the fires dimmed because the bellows blowers were not working hard enough, he would remind them of their duties by a blast from a cow horn. Now the lighthouse is to be automated and, it is hoped, will then pass from Trinity House to the care of the National Trust. [DN]

The underlying rocks of the Lizard Peninsula are of schist, gneiss, gabbro and serpentine. The last is a hard rock of reddish or greenish hue whose veiny texture reminded sixteenth-century geologists of the skin of a snake. Serpentine was once worked at Carleon Cove and, polished up, was used for fireplaces and ornamental urns. Today its use is reserved for small knick-knacks like model lighthouses, though stiles of serpentine can be found – and avoided in wet weather, when they become like ice.

This geology produces a rich and unusual botany, including the Cornish heath, a bright pink heather, the black bog rush, and very rare dwarf rushes. Some of the flora can be seen in the foreground of this photograph (*above*) in the traditional Cornish hedge that the Trust has built in local stone to overcome severe congestion of the road to Lizard Point. Pedestrians can now walk in safety along a parallel lane, leaving the road to wheeled transport. [DN]

CAPE CORNWALL, the only cape in England, lies just four miles north of Land's End. It was given to the Trust by H.J. Heinz and Co. Ltd in 1987, as commemorated in a small plaque in the shape of a baked beans tin label set into the granite base of the chimney that can be seen on the headland. [JC]

WEST PENWITH seems to be a wild, isolated landscape, but reveals centuries of settlement: prehistoric field systems, cliff castles and burial mounds, engine houses and tin mines. Just to the north of Cape Cornwall is the mining town of St Just.

Over the past ten years, the Enterprise Neptune Appeal has helped the Trust to acquire some four miles of this coastline, thus protecting such beautiful areas as Kenidjack, Bollowall and Nanjulian Farm, and preserving important features such as the Levant Beam Engine. Until 1991, when the last mine closed, the rugged coast and moorland had been mined for tin and copper for over 2,000 years, and the remoteness of the area has enabled this extraordinary mining landscape to escape the pressures of development, instead decaying gently back into the 'natural scenery'. [JC]

Looking down from Carn Galver towards BOSIGRAN FARM and the sea. The landscape of West Penwith is granite, giving a black soil that is surprisingly productive. Over the centuries farmers have painstakingly cleared their small fields and built up excellent holdings of beef cattle. The Trust encourages the tenant at Bosigran to continue to farm organically, grazing his livestock on the coastal heathland. [JC]

The seaside town of ST IVES. In 1939 the sculptress Barbara Hepworth set up her studio in St Ives and found her inspiration in Penwith: 'I gradually discovered the remarkable pagan landscape which lies between St Ives, Penzance and Land's End; a landscape which still has a very deep effect on me, developing all my ideas about the relationship of the human figure in landscape – sculpture in landscape and the essential quality of light in relation to sculpture which induced a new way of piercing the forms to contain colour.' Other artists, such as painters Ben Nicholson, Peter Lanyon and Patrick Heron, and the potter Bernard Leach, joined her, creating the Penwith Society of Arts. [JC]

Above: In *The Making of the English Landscape* W.G. Hoskins wrote that Cornwall was 'the most appealing of all industrial landscapes of England, in no way ugly, but indeed possessing a profound melancholy beauty.' The roofless engine house and stack of the tin mine at WHEAL COATES, perched on the cliff-top above the narrow cleft of Chapel Porth. [JC]

Right: PORT QUIN, one of the centres for pilchard fishing in the nineteenth century. [JC]

Pilchards, known as Fair Maids of Cornwall, a corruption of the Spanish *fumedos* or smoked, represented an important industry for the West Country. But in the 1870s seine fishing collapsed, partly due to fall in demand, partly a change in movements of the fish.

  When the pilchard industry was at its height, huge numbers of fish were dumped in the rectangular courtyards of fish cellars here and at Port Gaverne. Women 'bulkers' working at top speed would stack them between layers of salt along the cellar walls with their heads pointing outwards to a height of about five feet. The fish would remain like this for a month before being pressed into barrels.

Classic north Cornish coastal landscape at PENTIRE HEAD. Constantly exposed to the Atlantic gales, the rugged headland supports hardy moorland vegetation.

Left: Pentire Farm, with the Rumps in the distance. A local outcry took place in 1936 when the farm was divided into building plots and put up for sale. A photograph was published in *The Times* and a benefactor was found to underwrite the appeal until the money was raised to save it. [JC]

Above: The view west from Pentire Head to Stepper Point across the Camel Estuary, with Trevose Head beyond. [JC]

Above: Pentire Head, showing the Rumps, a tiny peninsula projecting from the northern corner. The neck of the peninsula provides a defensible site: in the Iron Age a castle was built here, and its fortifications can still be clearly picked out as bumps in the turf.

The walk out to the Rumps is one of the classics of the Cornish coast, the lie of the land changing with every step. Proceeding on to Pentire Point the greenstone and shale give way to pillow lava, the product of volcanic action millions of years ago. Here the walker is rewarded with stunning views. [JC]

Right: The rugged coast stretching from Padstow to Hartland contains only one natural haven, the fishing village of BOSCASTLE. Entering its harbour is still a hair-raising exprience on all but the calmest days. Sailing vessels could not get through the narrow strait without assistance from 'hobblers', boats with eight oars and men on either shore using guide ropes to keep them in mid-channel.

The inner jetty was rebuilt in 1584 by Sir Richard Grenville, the Elizabethan adventurer of *Revenge* fame. The outer jetty was blown up by a mine in 1941 but rebuilt after the harbour and its buildings was acquired by the National Trust. [JC]

Above: BARRAS NOSE, the headland north of King Arthur's Castle at Tintagel. This was the first piece of English coast to be acquired by the National Trust in 1897, as a result of widespread concern about the number of houses and hotels springing up in Tintagel because of the Arthurian connections. One manifestation was the monumental King Arthur's Castle Hotel, built by the London and South West Railway. Almost all the vernacular buildings in Tintagel disappeared at this time, with the exception of the Old Post Office, a delightful fourteenth-century open hall house that was rescued by the Trust in 1903. [JC]

Right: Strangles Beach at CRACKINGTON HAVEN. Sinister by name and sinister by nature, for the waters of the Atlantic pour into the narow inlet at high tide, cutting off the escape of those who have tarried too long. [JC]

Overleaf: Low tide at dusk, Strangles Beach. The rock at Crackington is a particular type of shale. Wildly contorted by movement of the earth's crust millions of years ago, it is easily fractured causing land-slips. To the left can be seen the screes leading up to a weird middle cliff of humps and bumps. [JC]

Joe Cornish was born and educated in Devon, before studying fine arts at Reading University. He worked as photographic assistant first to Mike Mitchell in Washington, and then with Dave Hart and Dale McAfee in London. His first 'clients' were actors and musicians for whom he did promotional portraits, but his customer list now includes many book publishers, magazines and organisations such as the Countryside Commission, the Cleveland Wildlife Trust and the Heritage Lottery Fund. The first book to which he contributed the photography was *Founders of the National Trust* published by Christopher Helm. He has also worked on books about France, Italy, and several guidebooks for Dorling Kindersley. He now lives in North Yorkshire.

Originally inspired by family holidays spent on the north Cornish coast, he has come particularly to enjoy photographing landscapes. The work of American masters like Ansel Adams and Edward Weston has given him a reverence for nature and in particular unspoilt, wilderness areas. Britain, in fact, is virtually wilderness free, but he identifies the coast below the high-tide mark as offering an authentic taste of untamed nature, where the ebb and flow of the sea will always resist man's efforts to domesticate. The ancient mountain landscapes of western and northern Britain evoke for him a sense of age and history combined with textural and colour subtlety that is often absent from younger, higher mountain ranges, such as the European Alps.

Joe decided he would like to work for the National Trust's Photographic Library after his involvement in the book on the founders. To celebrate the twenty-fifth anniversary of the launch of the coastal appeal, Enterprise Neptune, in 1990 the Trust commissioned the writer Charlie Pye-Smith to write *In Search of Neptune*, and Joe took the photographs. Since then he has travelled all over England, Wales and Northern Ireland for the Trust: 'To me, the Trust's landscape work is a force for our current benefit and for that of future generations. It follows therefore, that I feel my job is to express that work in the most evocative and positive way possible. Whenever I can, I take my photographs at dawn or dusk, exploiting the beautiful light conditions which tend to arise then if the weather is right.'

He started with 35mm SLRs, and still uses 35mm - he has Nikons with a range of lenses - but tends to limit their use to documentary-style portraits and general travel subjects. For landscape photographs he originally bought a second-hand Rolleicord twin lens reflex 6x6 (medium format) camera, replaced first by a Rolleiflex SLX single lens reflex, and then by a Pentax 6x7. Experience taught him to have extremely tough, reliable gear - the Pentax, for instance, stopped working after a close encounter with a large wave on the Cobb at Lyme Regis in Dorset. By 1986 therefore he had come down to two cameras, a Hasselblad 500CM and a Plaubel 69W Proshift, a fixed lens wide-angle camera with a built-in shift frame, and has used these ever since for his National Trust work. He continues to experiment and is currently working with a Horseman 612 camera for landscape work.

In the 1970s Kodachrome 64 (&25) was virtually *de rigueur* for anybody shooting 35mm. As it wasn't available in medium format film, he used Ektachrome 64 and later Fujichrome 50, until the arrival of Fuji Velvia in 1990. It is intolerant of exposure error, however, and slower than the 50 ASA stated. For shorter exposure and late twilight he uses Provia 100.

David Noton

David Noton was born in Bedfordshire but emigrated soon after to California. A peripatetic childhood spent in the UK and Canada was followed by a career in the Merchant Navy. His interest in photography began at sea, and in 1982 he returned to college in Gloucester. During his final year he sold Athena a range of images for publication as posters, which proved a springboard for going freelance. Initially his work was a balance of landscape and local commercial commissions for advertising agencies, design groups and public relations companies in the west country, from his Bristol base. By the 1990s his main activity was stock photography in the fields of landscape, nature and travel, and clients included NatWest, the National Grid, Ikea, the BBC Natural History Unit and the National Trust. He has won awards in the landscape categories of the British Gas/BBC Wildlife Photography Competition in 1985, 1990 and 1991. He is now based in Sherborne, Dorset.

As a keen walker and mountaineer, landscape photography was perhaps a natural preference which has endured. The Scottish Highlands and Islands were where his earliest photographic forays took place, and is still one of his favourite places. He relishes the ambience and unpredictability of field-work.

Despite, or perhaps as a result of travelling all over the world, David appreciates the wealth of differing landscapes - from dramatic mountain ranges to pastoral rolling farmland - offered by the British Isles. Because of the northerly latitude and the changeable weather, the subtlety of the light is unique. Man's imprint on the landscape, for instance the dry-stone walling and farm buildings in the Yorkshire Dales, adds visual harmony: 'Straight off the plane from, say, North America the patchwork of green fields still hits me between the eyes.'

The National Trust's Photographic Library is his longest running client, a relationship that started in 1986. The organisation is an obvious port of call for a photographer as it manages some of the most beautiful landscapes in Britain. 'To be able again and again to experience nature at its most enchanting at dawn on Derwentwater in the Lakes, or as storm waves crash on the rugged coast of the Lizard Peninsula in Cornwall brings home in no uncertain terms what a treasure we have in our landscape. I am committed to the work the Trust does in protecting these areas, and if in a small way my photographs help with that mission, it gives me great satisfaction.'

In the past ten years, David has used a whole range of equipment, but lately his set-up is Nikon 35mm gear and a Fuji 6x17cm panoramic camera. He is committed to the flexibility of 35mm, while appreciating the more considered but less spontaneous approach of working on the large 617 format. Virtually all his colour work is shot on Fuji Velvia.

Paul Wakefield

Paul Wakefield was born in Hong Kong, educated there and in the UK, and studied photography at Bournemouth and Birmingham Colleges of Art. He started his career as a photographer by freelancing for publishers, design groups and record companies while still at college. He now works mainly in advertising, with clients like car companies, British Gas, Smirnoff and Johnnie Walker. His exhibitions include the Photographers' Gallery in 1984, Gallery of Photography Dublin in 1991 and the Saatchi Gallery in 1994. Publications include three collaborations with Jan Morris on the landscapes of Wales, Scotland and Ireland. In 1997 he was given the Gold Award from the Association of Photographers. His studios are based in London.

Paul's interest in landscape stems from walking in the Hong Kong countryside with his father and brothers. He spends as much time as possible photographing for himself, and has most recently been working in Patagonia and the United States. He began working with the National Trust's Photographic Library about five years ago.

For cameras he uses a Linhof 5x4, Fuji 6x17/ 6x9 and a Leica M6. For colour film he uses Fuji Velvia, and for black and white shots, Agfapan 25/100.

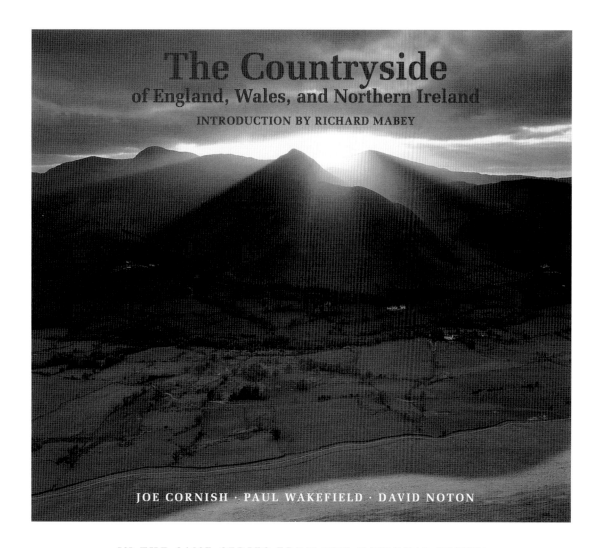

The Countryside
of England, Wales, and Northern Ireland
INTRODUCTION BY RICHARD MABEY

JOE CORNISH · PAUL WAKEFIELD · DAVID NOTON

IN THE SAME SERIES FROM THE NATIONAL TRUST:

Countryside

A photographic tour around the countryside of England, Wales and Northern Ireland,
as seen through the lenses of three leading landscape photographers:
Joe Cornish, David Noton and Paul Wakefield, with an introduction by Richard Mabey.
ISBN 0-8109-6361-2

Photographic books on gardens and historic house interiors
are planned for publication in 1999.

About the National Trust

The National Trust is Europe's leading conservation charity, looking after over 673,000 acres (272,000 ha) of countryside, 570 miles of coastline, 263 historic houses and 233 gardens and parks in England, Wales and Northern Ireland. The Trust continually requires funds to meet its responsibility of maintaining all these properties for the benefit of the nation. To find out how you can help, please contact:

The National Trust, 36 Queen Anne's Gate, London, SWIH 9AS (0171 222 9251).

Enterprise Neptune

Since 1965 when this special appeal was launched, the Enterprise Neptune campaign has acquired some of the finest – and often most vulnerable – coastal areas of England, Wales and Northern Ireland for permanent preservation by the National Trust. For more information contact:

The Enterprise Neptune Office, Attingham Park, Shrewsbury, Shropshire SY4 4TP (01743 709 343).

Membership

Joining the National Trust will give you free entry to properties and directly funds the Trust's work. For details of how to join, contact:

The National Trust Membership Department, PO Box 39, Bromley, Kent BRI INH (0181 315 1111).

Legacies

Please consider leaving the Trust a legacy in your will. All legacies to the National Trust are used either for capital expenditure at existing properties or for the purchase or endowment of new property – not for administration. For more information contact:

The Head of Legacies Unit, 36 Queen Anne's Gate, London SWIH 9AS (0171 222 9251).

The Royal Oak Foundation

This US not-for-profit membership organisation supports the National Trust's activities in areas of special interest to Americans. For membership and programme information in the US contact:

The Royal Oak Foundation, 285 West Broadway, New York, NY 10013 USA (00 1 212 966 6565).